for Dad

Oliver Emanuel

THE 306: DUSK

OBERON BOOKS
LONDON

WWW.OBERONBOOKS.COM

First published in 2018 by Oberon Books Ltd
521 Caledonian Road, London N7 9RH
Tel: +44 (0) 20 7607 3637 / Fax: +44 (0) 20 7607 3629
e-mail: info@oberonbooks.com
www.oberonbooks.com

PB ISBN: 9781786826282
E ISBN: 9781786826305

Cover image: Christopher Bowen
Cover design: Dill Design

10 9 8 7 6 5 4 3 2 1

Contents

Characters

RACHEL, *a teacher from London, black, 30s.*

KEITH, *a retired soldier, from Glasgow,*
any race, late 30s, early 40s.

PRIVATE LOUIS HARRIS OF 10TH WEST YORKSHIRE'S,
from Leeds, white, executed aged 23.

Also a choir of veterans, school children, the relatives of the lost,
as well as the dead and forgotten.

Part 1 is to be performed by any of the company taking
whatever lines they wish. The asterisks of Part 2 mark a
change of tone and/or energy but the monologues are
continuous. **Lines in bold are sung**. ***Lines in bold italic**
are sung by the choir.* The list in Part 3 should be sung
and/or projected on a screen.

Setting

11 November 2018. A wood in the Somme region of France.

A dash (–) indicates an interruption.
An ellipsis (…) indicates a trailing away or a thought-pause.
A Phrase With Capitals Indicates Emphasis.
(A word or phrase in parenthesis is thought but not uttered.)

Small clouds gathered and rain began to sprinkle on the dead, the wounded, the frightened, and the exhausted and on the doubtful men.

It was as if it were saying: "Enough, enough, men. Stop now… Come to your senses. What are you doing?"

War & Peace by Leo Tolstoy

1.

*He wakes up after 100 years, in the middle of
a wood.*

Shivering. Fearful. Blind.

There's no light.

*Yes there is light, just not much of it, not sun,
but a lightening of the dark.*

Dawn.

*He jumps as a crow takes off from an unseen
branch, scattering the silence.*

*He lies, half-buried, within and between
the roots of an ancient hornbeam. He's in
considerable pain. Stiff and brittle. He checks
himself over. Hands. Head. Arms. Legs. Feet.
Everything is present and correct, thank God.
His entire body is encased in mud and wetness
– sweat, dew, vomit, blood – he has no idea.
He has seven round holes in his shirt. The wind
whistles right through him.*

*He gets to his feet. There's no sign of another
soul. He closes his eyes and listens but the*

*darkness frightens him so he opens his eyes
again. Everything feels close in the half-light.
He smells something burning far away.*

A church-bell?

That's not possible.

First the crow now this.

*He can't remember how long it's been since he
heard these sounds.*

*And that's when it occurs to him, it dawns
on him, you might say, as the dawn steps
slowly through the trees and across the ground,
giving shape to the world that was previously
only blackness, it dawns on him that he has
absolutely no idea where he is.*

Or who he is.

He can't remember his name.

*He can't –
He can't remember –*

Sweat breaks out on his forehead.

He opens his mouth to scream but it's full of cobwebs.

He holds up his hands in front of his face. Hard and cracked like dry wood. He tries to recall something, anything that these hands have done, but he can't.

Alone in a wood, freezing, exhausted, starving. No memory of who he is or what he is doing. No clue as to what he should do next.

What happened?

Someone must have hit him. Yes. He must have been in a fight. Or he fell over, knocked himself against a tree branch. Possibly there was an explosion of some kind.

There was violence, he is sure.

He watches the light brighten in the canopies of the trees and listens to the crows.

There's something off about this place, something wrong.

It's more silent and still than a wood has a right to be.

More like a church.

Or a cemetery.

*He sees that he is a soldier. He is wearing
a soldier's uniform and soldier's boots. But
instead of feeling reassured by this fact, he
has only questions. What war am I fighting?
Where is my regiment? Where are my mates?
What happened to my weapon? What
happened? What happened?*

*He notices that he knows the names of trees.
Oak. Lime. Beech. That's something, at least.*

*He rests his hand against the broad trunk of
an oak tree.*

*There's a song too, a random melody, the rise
and fall, on the tip of his tongue. He believes
that if he can somehow remember the song that
everything else will reappear.*

He gives up.

He punches the oak tree and says fuck.

*It's his first word in a long time and he scares
himself half to death.*

*He says it again to make sure he wasn't
imagining it.*

The light grows every minute.

*As the sun rises to meet him, as the first rays
of day hit him in the face with the force of
a slap – no warmth in the light just colour,
yellow, cold, unforgiving – it's then that he
remembers –*

*He remembers he is dead.
He remembers –
He remembers everything.*

2.1

RACHEL: First thing I do when I wake up is check the news on my phone.

A mistake.

Nuclear threats. An unstoppable wildfire burning a hole in the atmosphere. Fucking Trump. Fucking Brexit.

I know I should relax.
I know I should be stronger.
I know I should block out the noise and the violence of everything.

The baby is kicking and I desperately need a piss.

I have the feeling that something is about to break.

*

I lead the kids into the woods and have them line up beside the memorial.

The veterans form similar ranks opposite.

Medals tinkle like rain on glass.

You can tell how old each regiment is
by height. The younger, more recent
soldiers are big, upright. The older ones
bent and small.

They seem to be having a smashing time.

Chatting, back-slapping, telling jokes.

It's a party!

One by one the kids fall silent as they
observe the soldiers.

They've never seen real soldiers before.

Not what they imagined.

Not big, brave, bloody heroes.

Their ordinariness is astonishing.

These are ordinary men and women
whose job it once was to fight for
their country.

The day is bleak. The sun hides in the canopies of the trees.

A corporal with 3 shiny medals and a giant embroidered poppy over her heart hands out the order of service on bits of card.

The card has suggestions for things to think about during the 2-minute Silence – silence with a capital S:

We Remember Those Who Gave Their Lives In Service To Their Country.

We Pray That We May Be Worthy Of Their Sacrifice.

We Pray For Peace.

I'm cold. A bit fed up. Since we got to France, we've already had 2 passports lost, 3 fights, 2 acts of heavy petting and this morning we found that 4 of the girls had spent the night getting drunk on a bottle of Calvados stolen from the hotel bar. What is it about school trips? These are beautiful, intelligent, sensitive kids. *In the classroom.* In the classroom, they are a total joy. Put them on a coach and they lose their fucking minds.

Something is about to break.

I feel eyes on me.

I turn but there's no one, nothing but trees and more trees. It's probably just my anxiety. I try to breathe but then the cannon goes off and the Silence begins.

Silence screams.

In the absence of words, I feel the pressure of everything bearing down on me.

It's too much.

I can't handle it.
I can't –

I break.

I don't plan it.
I don't ask permission.
I don't make any kind of excuse.

I just run.

*

I'm a good runner.

I did the London Marathon last year.

Not fast.

It's not the time that matters, it's
the finishing.

I wouldn't finish now.

It's a lot harder to run a marathon when
you're 32 weeks pregnant.

I have this app on my phone which tells
me the size of the baby compared to
vegetables. Right now, the baby is the size
of a head of lettuce.

I run with the lettuce away from the
memorial into the woods, as far and as
deep as I can. I need to get away, I –

I find a trench, scramble into it.

I look back.

There's no one and nothing following.

What I do next is not a conscious
decision. I don't make a choice. It just
happens, like I'm watching a film
of myself.

I take my phone out of my pocket and
smash it under my heel.

No going back.

*

When I discover I'm pregnant, I burst
into tears.

My partner thinks they're tears of joy.

I don't tell him otherwise.
I don't tell him that I'm absolutely terrified.
I don't tell him I'm scared of what the
future might bring.

He opens a bottle of champagne.

*

I wake up and you are in my bed.

I get up.
I wash.
I dress.
I go out.

You follow me everywhere.

You wait.
You listen.
You kick.
You cry.

You follow me everywhere.

I have to make good decisions.
If I don't, I know I'm not the only
one who will suffer.

*

I'm on the run.
Absent Without Leave.
A fugitive.

This is a criminal act of desertion.

If I'm caught, I could lose my job.
I could be shot.

I picture the Head and the other teachers
searching the memorial, the car park,
trying my phone, getting no answer.
The confusion on their faces.

I'm completely aware of the madness of
what I'm doing, the irresponsibility of it,
the selfishness.

I'm also completely aware that I don't
give a shit.

I feel free.

*

I take a deep breath.
I let my heart rate slow.

I put my hand out to steady myself on
the root of a tree.

I try to remember its name.

HARRIS: **Ash.**

Beech.

The mighty oak.

The sycamore tree.

Holly.

Cherry.

Lime.

Yew.

Hornbeam.

Hazel.

Poplar.

Pine.

RACHEL: Trees have excellent names.

Grandad taught me.

Grandad taught me the names of trees,
how to whistle and how to use a knife.

He showed me which parts of the body I
should attack if I wanted to cause the most
damage. The neck. The gut. The groin.

Grandad seemed very ordinary.

To look at Grandad, you'd never know
he was a trained killer.

Except for the walk.

There's a way soldiers walk, a step, the rhythm, that is beaten into them through repetition, it's unmistakable.

I could always tell when Grandad was coming from the sound of his boots.

Trees were the only thing Grandad truly loved.

He found human beings impossible.

He called me a loud, lazy bitch.

To be fair, Grandad said that about everyone who was born in the latter half of the twentieth century. He said that we were a massive disappointment, that if his generation had known what the future would hold they wouldn't have fucking bothered.

He loved swearing too.

I called him the Miserable Old Bastard.

Grandad said that trees were better than humans. They didn't disappoint and couldn't talk back. He liked the silence of trees.

When Grandad went weird later on – when the panic attacks were at their worst – the only thing that would calm him was to take him to the tree at the bottom of the garden.

I'd push him out on his special chair and he'd lay his hand against the thick ridges of bark.

His breathing slowed.

His chest relaxed.

The lines of his face unfurrowed.

After a while, he'd swear about catching his death but for that minute, it was like he was a proper Grandad.

Kind and gentle and odd.

*

I tell my kids there are all kinds of history.

Political. Military. Personal. Sexual. Family.
Medical. Internet. Criminal.

History is the measure of things.
History tells us where we come from and
where we will go.
History is past tense but also present tense.
Also future tense.
We went to war.
We are at war.
We will go to war.
History is not easy.

History is an act of the imagination.
You do not study history, you imagine it.

*

I want you to be happy.
I want you to be safe.
I want you to have friends.
I want you to find love.
I want you to dream.
I want you to like me.
I want you to be good.

*

A Personal History Lesson.

Grandad was my mum's dad.

He was born in 1895. He died in 2001.

He lived for 106 years which even he conceded was too long.

He left school at 15 to apprentice as a joiner. He built furniture.

He volunteered in 1916 and served 2 years on the Western Front in the 10th West Yorkshire's.

Married 4 times.

10 kids.

All of them hated him.

I was 13 when he came to live with us.

He'd been kicked out of the nursing home for repeated racist remarks.

He wasn't racist.

I mean, he *was* racist. He was terrible to
my dad. But he hated everyone. It wasn't
discrimination, it was misanthropy.

I loved him probably because no one
else did.

We'd drink Strongbow together in the
evenings. He gave me my first cigarette.

Although sometimes living with
the Miserable Old Bastard felt like
punishment for a crime I hadn't
committed.

He never spoke about the War.

He never wore a poppy or attended a
Remembrance Day service.

I never asked why.

A mistake. I didn't see how it was relevant
to me. I didn't see how who he'd been
had any effect on who I would become.

Here's my conclusion: good history is
about asking good questions.

*

I'm afraid you will be sad.
I'm afraid you will be in danger.
I'm afraid you'll be unhappy in love.
I'm afraid you won't aspire.
I'm afraid you will be lonely.
I'm afraid you will hate me.
I'm afraid you will be bad.

*

The inside of a tree reveals its entire history.

Cut it open and read its story.

We are different.

A human's remains only tell us so much.
It's an incomplete narrative.

Hold a human heart in your hand, it's
impossible to tell how well it loved.

*

If Grandad had been a tree, he'd have
been an oak.

Massive.

English.

Ancient.

I find an acorn on the ground.

It's perfect.

Whole.

But cold.

I warm it in my hand.

I try to imagine the tree it will become.

*

Will you have his eyes?
Will you have his look?
Will you be kind?
Will you know true friendship?
Will you betray someone?
Will you learn to forgive?

*

The rings inside a tree record its growth every year.

A warm, wet year, the ring is wide.

A cold, dry year is narrow.

1918 was cold, damp, foggy.

The tree remembers.

*

Grandad never spoke about the war but as he got older he lacked the strength to keep the memories at bay.

I read that can happen to old soldiers.

They spend their entire lives repressing their experiences, holding themselves in check, then one day it's right there in front of them.

*

It's dusk.

The light is failing fast.

I'm 18 years old, just back from dinner
at a mate's. I can hear Grandad sobbing
through the bedroom wall. I bang my fist
a few times but he won't shut up.

What's the problem, Miserable Old
Bastard? Pissed yourself again?

This is our little joke.

He likes it when I'm coarse but he's
always had a cast-iron bladder.

Grandad is sitting on the edge of his
bed, a shivering silhouette against the
open window.

He'd once been massive but his incredible
old age has shrunk him so that he's
smaller than me.

What's wrong with you?

Grandad opens his fist to show me
a photograph.

Black and white.

Hard to make out in the gloom.

I hold it up to the last of the sunlight.

A young man. A soldier in uniform. Smart
with a rigid centre parting. He's leaning
on a box, cocky as you please. I like
him instantly.

The photograph is faded but his
personality flashes out.

His name was Louis. He was my best
mate, Grandad says. We were at school
together. We joined up in '16 together.

What happened?

I killed him.

That's what he says. Just like that.

I had orders. I thought it was the right
thing to do, I –

I don't know what to say to that.

I don't say anything.

In fact, I smile.

It's a joke, right? You're joking.

But he looks at me.

Tears, snot, infinite loss in his beautiful,
big eyes.

You killed him? Your best mate…?

I wait for him to explain. To say
something, anything to make sense of it.

He doesn't say anything.

I know I should comfort him somehow.
I want to comfort him. But the distance
between us, from where I'm standing and
him on the bed, is growing, widening
and stretching by the second, and I don't
know how to make the leap.

I break.

I go through the door, down the stairs,
head out into the street and don't
look back.

I run.

I don't understand it but I want to get as far away as I can.

Fuck.

I stay at a mate's house that night and don't come back 'til morning. When I do, Grandad's dead.

Heart attack, apparently.

I don't believe it.

I know I killed him.

We remember.

We remember you.

We remember your eyes.

*We remember your touch and the way you
looked when you thought you were alone.*

We remember what made you shout.

We remember what made you cry.

We remember all the little things.

*We remember the light of you.
The dark of you.*

We remember that's been a long time.

We remember it's forever.

KEITH: Throughout history, the best fighter,
        the most violent male survives to pass
        on his genes.

        Peace and understanding are well
        and good.

        That's not the way the world works.

        Some folks call them psychos.

        Others, heroes.

        Personally, I call them Natural Cunts.

        It's always the main bloke in the action
        film – James Bond, Jason Bourne,
        Bruce Willis.

        The cool, calm killer.

        Your Natural Cunt can control his fear.
        Your Natural Cunt loves the brotherhood
        of the fighting unit.
        Your Natural Cunt welcomes the boredom
        of day-to-day soldiering.

It's not that he loves to kill.

He'll only kill when he has good reason.

Like in a war.

What sets your Natural Cunt apart from his fellow soldiers is that he feels no remorse, no regret.

To him, killing is a rational act.

When the war is over, your Natural Cunt re-enters society no bother.

The problem is, Natural Cunts are incredibly rare.

In all my years of professional soldiering, I only met 2.

Maybe 3.

You don't know what you are 'til you (get home) –

*

2 tours in Iraq. 3 in Afghanistan.

I come home without a scratch.

I got pals – Paul, Tommy, JJ – who never make it back.

I'm one of the lucky ones.

But that first night, I start telling my wife about What It Was Like out there, the things that had happened, the people and that but she tells me to shut up.

Let's call her…Sophie.

Not her real name but whatever.

Shut up, says Sophie.

She says, no one wants to hear about that here.

No one is interested.

There are other things happening in the world.

Sophie used to love hearing my war stories. She used to find them sexy. She used to show off about me to her pals.

We've moved on, Keith. You need to move on too.

And even though she's smiling when she says it, the look on Sophie's face is more angry and like she wants this conversation to end.

I don't know what to say.

So I say nothing.

We talk about how the dishwasher is broken and we need to get (a new one) –

*

His smile.
His face.

His smile.
His face.

*

But, you know, Paul was a top bloke.

We did Basic together.

Took our Sergeant's exam at the
same time.

We always swore we'd look out for
each other's family if the worst came to
the worst.

I put off seeing his missus for a month.

She's gonna ask questions and I don't
have any answers.

When I eventually go to her house, she
calls me a Coward and spits in my face.

Slams the door.

I go home, lock myself in the bog and
have a wee cry.

I say nothing.

*

The only people who know why I'm
invalided out are me and the doctor.

I try to tell some pals but no one wants
to know.

Everyone acts like I've been away on
holiday.

You look tanned, they say. Where've you
been? Lanzarote.

I get into a fight at my local with a student
who says the British intervention in Iraq
was a War Crime.

What the fuck do you know about it?
I say.

I knock him out cold.

It takes 4 cops to get me out of the pub.

I'm totally raging.

My old CO bails me out.

When we're leaving the police station he
calls me a fucking disgrace.

You need to sort yourself out, Keith.

*

I did the right thing.

I did the right thing.

I did the right thing.

*

Aye I'm barred from the pub so I have to drink at home.

6 cans of lager. 1 bottle of wine. Half-bottle of whisky.

Every night.

I feel like shite in the morning but at least I don't remember the Dreams.

The Dreams, man.

I'm telling you, they're so fucking (real) –

*

Sophie has all these magazines on the coffee table.

Best.
OK!
Take a Break.

I find them fascinating.

I like the celebrity gossip. The advice
page is shite.

Time heals fuck all.

Months go by.

I get fat.

I shout at strangers in supermarkets.

I experience blackouts. Whole minutes,
hours, when I don't know what's
going on.

We don't have sex for months.

When we go out, I have to sit in the
corner of the restaurant with my back to
the wall or I break into a sweat.

One Sunday, it takes me 3 hours to
get back from the shops with the gravy

granules cos I'm convinced I'm being followed.

What's wrong with you? Sophie asks.

I stare at her and her parents who've been sitting, watching their tea get cold.

I –

I say nothing.

I don't tell her I've been doubling back, taking buses in opposite directions across the city, running along the canal, checking the horizon for snipers.

HARRIS: **Ingram Street.**
Candleriggs.
Byres Road.
Rottenrow.
Buchanan Street.
Albert Road.
Drygate.
Saltmarket.

KEITH: Hypervigilance.

That's what it's called.

I look it up when her folks have gone home and Sophie's pouring gravy down the sink.

An enhanced state of sensory sensitivity which may bring about increased anxiety and fatigue.

There are links to mental health organisations.

What no fucking website will tell you is What You Should Do If You Are Actually Being Followed.

I see things that your average citizen wouldn't.

I've been trained.

There are bad people in the world.

There are bad people who want to hurt my country.

Sophie is my country too.

I must protect my country.

I must protect my country.

I Must Protect My (Country) –

*

His face.
His smile.
His face.
His smile.
His face.
His smile
His face.
His smile.

*

Killing another human being is the worst
thing you can do.

I firmly believe that.

But in the moment of killing, that's not
what you feel.

You feel exhilaration.

Joy.

It's called the Combat High.

The Combat High is like a big fucking
injection of heroin straight to the heart.

BOOM.

Blood-pounding.
Lung-pounding.

You float.
You laugh.

You are oblivious to Everything and
Everyone.

FUUUUUUUCCCCCKKKK!

The intensity.

Most soldiers won't tell you this.

No one wants to hear that killing is fun,
do they?

But the Combat High is just one stage
of killing.

The next stage is Remorse.

Remorse can last a long time…a lifetime.

You try to rationalise.

You try to tell yourself –

*

I Did The Right Thing.
I Did The Right Thing.
I Did The Right Thing.
I Did The Right Thing.
I Did The Right Thing.
I Did The Right Thing.
I Did The Right Thing.

*

Paul and I are at a crossroads in Helmand
when the wee lad with the wheelbarrow
shows up.

We've seen him before.

He's smiling.

50 yards off.

The atmospherics have been bad
all day. We're at the edge of a village.
It was bombed but reconstruction has
started. There are families and shops.
It's lunchtime. Usually, there's the smell
of cooking, the sound of chatter. None of
that. The locals won't come near.

We're on high alert.

We call to him to stop.

The lad keeps coming, the lad keeps smiling.

Paul shouts a final warning but it's too late
I've already pulled the trigger.

Paul gives me a look.

What the fuck?

The wheelbarrow has footballs in it but it
could've been anything.

I did the Right Thing.

I'd do it again.

That night, I can't sleep. I'm exhilarated.
Wired.

Next week Paul is taken out by an IED at
the same crossroads.

A Coincidence.

But I can't get it out of my head.

The wee lad's smile.
Paul's face.

I manage another couple of months
before the doctor says I've got anxiety
and that's that.

After 12 years in the Army, I'm out.

Fuck you very much.

*

I see his face.
His face.

I see his smile.
He smiles at me.

I close my eyes
and still he's there.

He's looking at me...why?
He's smiling at me...why?

Why? Why? Why? Why? Why?
Why? Why?

*

The night everything goes wrong
starts brilliantly.

I've been feeling much better.

Got things sorted in my head.

I have 3 routes to work. I roll a dice every
morning to decide which one to take.

I keep a spare passport under the
bathroom sink.

In the pocket of my jacket, I carry a
compact version of the SIG Sauer P226
known as the P228 that an Army pal
got me.

I love guns. I love the feel of them.
The texture of the grip. The weight.
The engineering on modern small arms
is out of this world.

Anyway, we have a top night.

Tea with Sophie's pals. Drinks after.
We skip home early to have sex for the
first time in forever.

It's dusk.

Magic time.

The light on our bodies is movie-light.
Perfect.

Oh God I love her so fucking much.

Even after 15 years, she is unbelievably
sexy to me.

We fall asleep in each other's arms as
night comes on.

Next thing I know, I'm standing over
Sophie's naked, unconscious body, the
short muzzle of the P228 shoved between

her lips, the bottom half of her jaw
hanging weird.

I've broken it.

Also her upper femur in her right leg.

Also 3 ribs.

Later the doctors find evidence of
repeated beatings to her stomach
and back.

What?

I must've been drunk when it happened
cos I –
I don't remember.

That's no excuse and I'm not trying to get
out of what I done but I –

I don't remember.

I cradle her in my arms 'til the ambulance
shows up.

She can't speak.

Neither can I.

I want to say something, make it right, but what's to say?

I hold her hand as she's wheeled into the operating theatre and that's the last time I see her.

When I go out into the corridor, the police are waiting for me and I'm like (what's happening?) –

*

Aye so yeah. After 3 years inside for Aggravated Assault and Possession Of An Illegal Firearm, I'm diagnosed.

Post-Traumatic Stress Disorder.

The doctor says it like I should be grateful.

You can start your life over again now, the doctor says.

Fuck that.

I liked my old fucking life.

I want it back.

FUCK.

I write Sophie a letter.

I tell her everything.

She doesn't write back.

We are forgotten.
We are unknown.
We are dead but not resting,
never at peace.
We are in the shadows.
We are in the mud.

No name.

Cut me out
cut me out
like a wart
like an eye.

I have no name.

HARRIS: I'm 8 days old.

Mam still can't decide on a name.

The Rabbi is trying to keep his temper.
The bris is less than 10 minutes away.

Everyone told her she'd know.

When you see your baby for the first time
you'll know, they said.

But here I am, bold as a bollock, and she's
none the wiser.

What's your name?

*

I'm 10 years old.

First day of a new school.

We've just moved to Leeds from down
south. I've spent the day repeating myself.
Most of the other kids have never heard
another accent before.

Now Alf has me against the playground wall.

Alf is massive. He has massive hands and massive arms and a massive head. He's only 6 months older but he might as well be 6 years. I can feel the points of his fingertips sharp in my shoulders.

I'm going to kill you, fucking yid.

I never heard the name before but I can tell it's not good.

I feel like crying and shitting myself at the same time but I hear Mam whispering in my ear. Never show the bastards you're afraid.

So I kick Alf in the bollocks. I stamp on his foot. Leather. Flesh. Bone.

One of the teachers has to pull me off before I boot him in the face.

Next morning, Alf is waiting for me around the corner with a couple of big lads.

I don't run.

The big lads hold me down to let Alf take
his revenge.

I smile at him.

What you smiling at, fucking yid?

When I get home Mam cries and shouts
at me but I don't tell her anything.

I'm given no tea and packed off to bed.

But I'm back at school the next day.

Bruised, bloody but defiant.

Alf watches me from the back of
the classroom.

He knows the blow must come. That's
the law of nature as Alf sees it.

But it never does.

I show him I'm not afraid and keep
my trap shut.

Next week, Alf is waiting around the
corner again but this time he's alone and

he's got a toy soldier that his dad made
from some wood.

He hands it over and from then on we're
best mates.

Life's simple when you're 10 years old.

*

I'm 20 years old.

It's my birthday.

We're at the City Varieties.

Alf has bought us good seats.

I bloody love Music Hall.

Just before the interval, a young lady
dressed as a soldier sings a song about
bravery and fighting for King and
Country.

Alf wipes his eyes with his sleeve.

When the show's over, the young lady
is standing by the exit with a Recruiting
Sergeant.

She's all smiles and that smile. Bugger me.

Alf and me sign our names on the piece of
paper and Alf asks her out for a drink.

He's always had an eye for the lasses.

And they have an eye for him, big lad
that he is.

I say nothing.

Alf gives me a wink.

Bastard.

I know when I'm not wanted.

*

KEITH: **Ingram Street.**
            Candleriggs.
            Byres Road.
            Rottenrow.

Buchanan Street.
Albert Road.
Drygate.
Saltmarket.

HARRIS: All the trenches are named after streets
back home.

A sick joke.

I can barely remember what home
looks like.

The war is my home.

*

I'm an ordinary soldier.

Nothing special.

I know my serial number and my duties.

Sergeant calls my name and I'm there.

I march.
I clean my kit.
I reinforce trenches.

I dig latrines.

I go on patrol.

I play cards with Alf.

I write letters to Mam.

I dream of the future...of what happens
when the war is over.

*

I'm 22 years old.

Alf and I are volunteered for night patrol
with a replacement Lieutenant.

He's only been on the line for a week.

Why us?

Your names have been pulled out of a
hat, the Sergeant says with a grin. Fair
and square.

Generally, I like night patrols. The point
of night patrols is not to engage the
enemy. You're there to observe, make
a map. If you come across the enemy
your orders are to run like fuck. I like
the feeling of slipping over the top,

unobserved, in total darkness, cutting the
wire, crawling forward into danger. The
only sound the beating of your heart.
It's exciting.

We go over the plan 3 times, the
Lieutenant's hand shaking as he explains.

He looks terrified.

Nothing to be frightened of, I say like I
know what I'm talking about.

This patrol is an easy 50 yards across No
Man's Land. We're to make a note of the
enemy position, then straight home for
rum and medals. With any luck, we're
back within an hour.

The trench is supposed to be empty.

The look of surprise on the face of the
German when the 3 of us drop in front of
him. It's a picture.

He's frozen. He doesn't raise his rifle but
stares at us, mouth agape.

Alf and I turn to leg it but like a plonker
the Lieutenant pulls out his revolver.
Fuck. He's shaking so bad, he couldn't hit
a barn door.

Fritz comes to his senses.

I fire.

This is the first and last time I knowingly
kill another human being.

In battle, there's always so much smoke
and noise that it's impossible to tell.

I kneel down in the mud to look at
the German.

He's just a kid. Younger even than me.
Top half of his face is missing and he's
only got one eye. There's mud splashed in
his mouth and, for some reason, this is the
thing that bothers me most. I brush the
mud away with my sleeve.

I'm sorry, I tell him.

I'm so sorry.

*

I can't sleep.

I turn up late to drill.

I don't shave and get put on report.

I tell the CO to go fuck himself.

I weep for no reason, day or night.

I can't get the dead German lad out
my head.

I wish I knew his name.

*

I'm 22 years old.

We're attacking the village of Rocquigny.

We're not expecting much resistance.
The CO reckons Fritz has done a runner.

I'm in the team with the Lewis gun. We
pause to catch our breath for 5 minutes. I
drop my pack on the ground, lean against
a tree and smoke a cigarette that tastes of
nothing. It's strange but I've lost my sense
of taste. Everything tastes of mud.

When the break is over, the Sergeant calls
our names and the rest of the team head
off but I –

I stay where I am.

I pretend I haven't heard.

I watch them go.

I sit beneath the tree.

I put out my cigarette and walk in the
opposite direction.

*

This is a criminal act of desertion.

I don't know where I am or what
I'm doing.

It's madness.

I touch each tree as I pass, saying their
names out loud.

I feel free.

RACHEL: **Ash.**

Beech.

The mighty oak.

The sycamore tree.

Holly.

Cherry.

Lime.

Yew.

Hornbeam.

Hazel.

Poplar.

Pine.

HARRIS: After I'm caught, I'm charged with *misbehaving before the enemy in such a manner to show cowardice* as well as *deserting His Majesty's Army.*

At the Court Martial all I can see is the dead German lad's face.

He is the Colonel in charge.

He is the prosecuting counsel.

He is every witness.

I'm so ashamed.

I want to ask his forgiveness but I can't
find the words.
I want to but I –
I say nothing.

I offer no defence and refuse to have
anyone speak on my behalf.

They can't prove cowardice but they get
me for desertion so that's that.

I see the Colonel strike my name from a
list as I'm dragged from the room.

*

I'm chained to a railing in an old
cow barn.

Shit-stinking, bitter cold.

Alf comes to visit when he can.

We play cards.

We laugh, talk about home, the old days
at school, the lasses we like. Memories.

We don't talk about what is to come.

I like to believe that Alf knows everything
I'm thinking and I know everything he's
thinking.

We don't need words.

Love, I suppose you'd call it.

Except the last night, Alf doesn't come
and there are no goodbyes.

I write a note to Mam.

I tell her everything.

My hand shakes as I sign my name.

3.1

RACHEL: I'm an anxious person.

I wasn't always anxious but that's what
I've become.

Or what the world has made me.

Every day I read the news and ask myself:
what is happening?

I'm easily triggered.

I find it difficult to get perspective
on things.

Someone told me that I'd chill out when I
got pregnant but it hasn't happened yet.

Every day is a battle.

KEITH: I'm a changed man, I say.

Violence has changed me, I say. I know
how to kill but I don't know how to live.
I thought I was a Natural Cunt. That I
could make sense of the things that have

happened in the past, that I could move
on but –

Sophie is giving me a look.

She stands with the front door only open
a crack, the chain still on.

It's raining. I'm soaked through. I came
straight to hers when I got out of prison.
I've no coat.

And then she tells me that she can't
forgive me.

She can't forget.

I don't know what to say to that so I
say nothing.

Sophie closes the door.

I don't blame her.

I don't.

I just wish (it was different) –

RACHEL: When the Head asks for volunteers to
take the Year 11s to the Somme, I raise
my hand.

The last chance of a trip before the
baby comes.

Plus how can I call myself a Historian
without ever having gone to the
battlefields?

KEITH: I read in the newspaper about a Memorial
Service in the Somme.

I didn't get an invite.

My name has been crossed off the list,
forgotten.

Fuck it.

I'll go anyway.

ALL: **I have no name
no name.**

**Shot at dawn,
grave unmarked.**

I have no name.

Cut me out,
cut me out
like a wart
like an eye.

I have no name.
I have no name.

KEITH: But then when I'm here, I wish I'd
never come.

I can't stand it.

All these people.

Standing around and singing hymns and
talking about Heroes and shit.

I never met a Hero in my life.

What about cunts like me?

Ordinary Cunts.

Broken Cunts.

Cunts Who Don't Know Which Way Is Up.

No one gives me a second glance.

It's like I'm invisible.

RACHEL: I think about Grandad every day.

He's part of me, my history.

I wish there were some way for me to make amends.

For both of us.

KEITH: I piss off into the wood.

I feel violent.

I don't know how long I walk.

I get completely lost.

RACHEL: I see a man standing beside a tree.

It's dusk.

The light is bad.

For a second I think it's (Grandad) –

The man is dressed like the other soldiers at the Memorial.

He has a medal on his chest.

And he's crying.

Big, heaving sobs.

His whole body is shaking.

I feel the urge to run.

KEITH: There are thousands of bodies buried in this wood.

I can hear them talking to me.

It's too much, man.

(The woods. Dusk. The dead rise from the earth, from behind trees and the shadows. They address one another and also RACHEL and KEITH. HARRIS is in amongst them.)

We are forgotten.

We are unknown.

**We are dead but not resting,
never at peace.**

We are in the shadows.

We are in the mud.

(KEITH wipes his eyes and addresses RACHEL directly. HARRIS listens.)

KEITH: But – but it's like I don't exist. Like I've been erased.

RACHEL: How's that?

KEITH: 100 years ago, the wankers would've shot me.

RACHEL: There are some things people would rather forget. I'm like that. If I can't handle something, I run away, pretend it never happened.

KEITH: I'm not a bad man. I'm not a coward. I failed but (who doesn't?) –

RACHEL: I'm scared to face the difficult things.

KEITH: I'm more than what happened that day. I'm more than a single moment.

RACHEL: I have to stop running.

KEITH: I'm more than that.

RACHEL: I want to remember the truth of what
            happened.

KEITH: The truth? What's that?

RACHEL: His name was Louis Harris. He was
            the last of the 306 to be executed by
            the British Army. 2 days before the end
            of the war.

KEITH: Fuck.

RACHEL: I want my child to know his name.
            It's our history.

KEITH: History is a bastard.

RACHEL: I want to remember all their names.

KEITH: *(To HARRIS.)* What's your name?

RACHEL: It's only with the names that history
            means anything at all.

            *

Louis Harris is 23 years old.

The sun is only a rumour when he's taken from the barn and tied to the hornbeam tree.

He's completely pissed.

He's been drinking solidly all night.

His knees are shaking and he wants to puke.

He doesn't want to die.

The CO sticks an envelope over his heart and orders him not to slouch.

7 blokes from the regiment line up, rifles at the ready.

The one at the end is Alf.

Alf is the last thing Louis sees before he's blindfolded.

He takes Alf in, all of him.

His eyes.

Alf has the most astonishingly beautiful eyes.

Louis has never noticed.

Fuck.

Alf is watching him with his beautiful eyes and there's fear and love and everything in between.

Louis wants to call out, tell Alf to give him a smile the miserable old bastard – like if he spoke it might make a difference to what is about to happen.

1. His name was Thomas. 2. His name was George. 3. His name was Edward. 4. His name was Archibald. 5. His name was Frederick. 6. His name was Joseph. 7. His name was George. 8. His name was Thomas. 9. His name was Albert. 10. His name was William. 11. His name was Andrew. 12. His name was Joseph. 13. His name was Albert. 14. His name was George. 15. His name was George. 16. His name was Alfred. 17. His name was Thomas. 18. His name was Ernest. 19. His name was James. 20. His name was William. 21. His name was Isaac. 22. His name was Joseph. 23. His name was William. 24. His name was William. 25. His name is unknown. 26. His name was Major. 27. His name was John. 28. His name was James. 29. His name was Oliver. 30. His name was George. 31. His name was Herbert. 32. His name was Thomas. 33. His name was Ernest. 34. His name was William. 35. His name was Thomas. 36. His name was William. 37. His name was Thomas. 38. His name was Fatoma. 39.

His name was Herbert. 40. His name was Alfred. 41. His name was John. 42. His name was Ernest. 43. His name was Frederick. 44. His name was Bert. 45. His name was Evan. 46. His name was Louis. 47. His name was Peter. 48. His name was George. 49. His name was James. 50. His name was Alexander. 51. His name was Arthur. 52. His name was William. 53. His name was Harry. 54. His name was James. 55. His name was Patrick. 56. His name was John. 57. His name was John. 58. His name was James. 59. His name was John. 60. His name was William. 61. His name was Robert. 62. His name was John. 63. His name was Alfred. 64. His name was James. 65. His name is unknown. 66. His name is unknown. 67. His name is unknown. 68. His name was Abraham. 69. His name was Harry. 70. His name was Fortunat. 71. His name is unknown. 72. His name was Edward. 73. His name was William. 74. His name was Henry. 75. His name was Anthony. 76. His name was William. 77. His name was James. 78. His name was Arthur. 79. His name was John. 80. His name is unknown. 81. His name was Albert. 82. His name is unknown. 83. His name was William. 84. His name was William. 85. His name was James. 86. His name is unknown. 87. His name was James. 88. His name was James. 89. His name was James. 90. His name was John. 91. His name was Griffiths. 92. His name was Frederick. 93. His name was George. 94. His name was John. 95. His name was James. 96. His name was Joseph. 97. His name is unknown. 98. His name was Arthur. 99. His name was James. 100. His name was Frederick. 101. His name was John. 102. His name was George. 103. His name was Bertie. 104. His name was Come. 105. His name was William. 106. His name was Frederick. 107. His name was Allan. 108. His name was Jesse. 109. His name was EJ. 110. His name was Peter. 111. His name was Frank. 112. His name was James. 113. His name was John. 114. His name was Arthur. 115. His name was Herbert. 116. His name was James. 117. His name was Charles. 118. His name was Joseph. 119. His name was Albert. 120. His name was James. 121.

His name was Peter. 122. His name was Edward. 123. His name was Aziberi. 124. His name was John. 125. His name was Thomas. 126. His name was James. 127. His name was Harry. 128. His name was Albert. 129. His name was Richard. 130. His name was Henry. 131. His name was Elsworth. 132. His name was Alfred. 133. His name was Bernard. 134. His name was Harry. 135. His name was Robert. 136. His name was John. 137. His name was William. 138. His name was Hugh. 139. His name was Alfred. 140. His name was William. 141. His name was Henry. 142. His name was George. 143. His name was Reginald. 144. His name was William. 145. His name was William. 146. His name was Alfred. 147. His name was Albert. 148. His name was John. 149. His name was John. 150. His name was Samuel. 151. His name was Harry. 152. His name was Ernest. 153. His name was Eric. 154. His name was Charles. 155. His name was Peter. 156. His name was Edwin. 157. His name was Joseph, better known as 'Willie'. 158. His name was John. 159. His name was Peter. 160.

His name was John. 161. His name was Frederick. 162. His name was James or Joseph. 163. His name was Robert. 164. His name was Ernest. 165. His name was James. 166. His name was Albert. 167. His name was William. 168. His name was Frederick. 169. His name was Robert. 170. His name was Thomas. 171. His name was Richard. 172. His name was Ellis. 173. His name was Frederick. 174. His name was John. 175. His name was William. 176. His name was Arthur. 177. His name was William. 178. His name was Fredrick. 179. His name was George. 180. His name was William. 181. His name was Eugene. 182. His name was John. 183. His name was Joseph. 184. His name was Harold. 185. His name was Allassan. 186. His name was Thomas. 187. His name was George. 188. His name was Samuel. 189. His name was Archibald. 190. His name was Charles. 191. His name was John. 192. His name is unknown. 193. His name was Arthur. 194. His name was James. 195. His name was Joseph. 196. His name was Walter. 197. His name was Gustave. 198. His name was

Robert. 199. His name was John. 200. His name was Robert. 201. His name was Edward. 202. His name was Harry. 203. His name was Denis. 204. His name was Frederick. 205. His name was William. 206. His name was George. 207. His name was Samuel. 208. His name was Frederick. 209. His name was Hubert. 210. His name was John. 211. His name was Frederick. 212. His name was Arthur. 213. His name was James. 214. His name was Stanley. 215. His name was Thomas. 216. His name was Albert. 217. His name was Walter. 218. His name was James. 219. His name was Joseph. 220. His name was John. 221. His name was Thomas. 222. His name was William. 223. His name was Charles. 224. His name was John. 225. His name was George. 226. His name was Leonard. 227. His name was Herbert. 228. His name was Henry. 229. His name was Ernest. 230. His name was John. 231. His name was Dimitro. 232. His name was Mahmoud. 233. His name was Thomas. 234. His name was Norman. 235. His name was Frederick. 236. His name was William. 237. His name was Frank. 238. His name was Thomas. 239. His name was Ernest. 240. His name was Frederick. 241. His name was William. 242. His name was Ernest. 243. His name was Charles. 244. His name was Stephen. 245. His name was Henry. 246. His name was Thomas. 247. His name was John. 248. His name was George. 249. His name was John. 250. His name was William. 251. His name was Richard. 252. His name was Thomas. 253. His name was Thomas. 254. His name was Ernest. 255. His name was Thomas. 256. His name was Arthur. 257. His name was James. 258. His name was Joseph. 259. His name was Frederick. 260. His name was Charles. 261. His name was Harry. 262. His name was John. 263. His name was Wilfred. 264. His name was Thomas. 265. His name was Ernest. 266. His name was Victor. 267. His name was Ernest. 268. His name is unknown. 269. His name was Hector. 270. His name is unknown. 271. His name was Arthur. 272. His name was Henry. 273. His name was Albert. 274. His name was James. 275. His name was Frank. 276.

His name was Robert. 277. His name was Leopold. 278. His name was John. 279. His name was Walter. 280. His name was Malcolm. 281. His name was William. 282. His name was Thomas. 283. His name was William. 284. His name was Stephen. 285. His name was Walter. 286. His name was David. 287. His name was Arthur. 288. His name was George. 289. His name was Harry. 290. His name was Frederick. 291. His name was Benjamin. 292. His name was William. 293. His name was John. 294. His name was William. 295. His name was William. 296. His name was Harry. 297. His name was Joseph. 298. His name was Frederick. 299. His name was Frank. 300. His name was Patrick. 301. His name was Robert. 302. His name was David. 303. His name was Harry. 304. His name was Lawrence. 305. His name was Ernest. 306. His name was Louis.

END OF PLAY

NOTE: The list of the 306 names is taken from several sources, including *Shot At Dawn* by Julian Putowski & Julian Sykes and *Blindfold And Alone* by Catherine Cons & John Hughes-Wilson. In some cases, it proved impossible to find a first name thus some are marked 'His name is unknown'. Any errors are my own.

Some of Keith's views on soldiering and killing are inspired by the work of Dave Grossman and Gwynne Dyer.

Acknowledgements

Thank you to Jackie, Brenna, Caroline, Eileen, Rosie, Laura, Maureen, Emma, Joe, Seth and everyone at the National Theatre of Scotland.

Thank you to Jenny and Emma and all at 14:18 NOW.

Thank you to Perth Theatre for being awesome partners and hosts of this big, mad project for the last 3 years.

Thank you to the brilliant Sam Tranter for his research.

Thank you to all the actors and musicians who helped develop this play and get it to where it is today.

Thank you to the actors and musicians of *Dawn* and *Day*, it was smashing.

Thank you to Laurie and Jemima for getting us to this point.

Thank you to Lewis Hetherington for great words at a great moment.

Thank you to Vickie and Matilda, and my family.

Thank you to the entire creative team – Cécile, Eddy, Jonathan, Lewis, Kai and Matt – you guys rock.

Thank you to our ace choir.

Thank you to Ryan, Danny and Sarah.

Thank you to Gav and the production team.

Thank you to Lu Kemp for service above and beyond.

Thank you to Wils Wilson for brilliance and hard work and scones.

And thank you to Gareth, my brother.

Extracts from *Diary Of A Play*

To the glory of God and in memory of the men who gave their lives in the world war.

In grateful remembrance of the men who fell.

Bithidh iad air chuimhne anns gach linn a thic.

Every village, town and city in the UK has a monument with words and lists of names of the fallen. Perhaps a few fresh flowers, plastic poppy wreaths.

I'm standing in a village in the West Highlands of Scotland, reading the dozen or so names of the local men who fought in the First World War.

Whenever I notice one of these monuments, large or small, I wonder how often people nowadays really take the time to read the names. Everyone who remembers that war is dead. These stone crosses, statues and cairns were built to remember men, husbands, fathers, sons, but I sometimes feel they are memorials to forgetting.

In 2018, what place do these hold in our memories?

3/1/18

Today is the first day of research. Well, not exactly. I've been reading and thinking about the First World War for almost 5 years now. I've got an entire bookcase of histories, novels and poems about 'the war to end all wars.' A lot of them have bits of paper sticking out of them, post-its, etc. One of them has a photocopy of the will of one of the executed men.

I've made a start today on research for the final part, *Dusk*. Notes from my researcher Sam are excellent – after 2 shows together, he knows the sort of thing I'm interested in – and I've made notes of his notes.

At this stage, I don't want to make any decisions. Everything needs to be up in the air. Even though the show is on in less than a year (gulp), I have to pretend that I have all the time in the world to play.

I shuffle a pack of story cards and see that 'death' is the first one.

I've also written a brief schedule of where we are going on our research trip to France. Gareth and I went in 2014 and took in as much as we possibly could of the Somme region. This time we're going with Wils Wilson (director), Seth Hardwick (video producer at NTS) and Matt Padden (sound designer) so we have to be more selective in our destinations. Thiepval, Delville Wood, Newfoundland Park, and the cemetery where the last executed man is buried are all on the list.

As well as reading, I find that actually going to the place I'm writing about is invaluable. I've written lots of plays about places I've never been but as Normandy is so close there's no reason not to go.

I can't wait, although I predict we will be freezing and wet most of the time.

Whose idea was it to go in January?

8/1/18

We landed in Paris late last night and drove through the night to get to Normandy. I knew the familiar landscape was out there, hidden in the dark. The woman at the hotel gave us peanuts and beer when we arrived.

We get up early to visit Newfoundland Park. This is a great place to start for those of us – Matt, Seth and Wils – who have never been to this region before. The site was bought by a priest and the widows of the Canadian soldiers who died here and so there are many perfectly preserved trenches of both the Allies and Germany.

There's a school party already in the park. A teacher stands in No Man's Land while the students listen with bored, cold faces in a trench. One of my characters in the play is a teacher so it feels like serendipity.

As we reach the German lines and look back, it's amazing how near the Allied lines were, how short a distance and what an insignificant piece of land was being fought over. Wils, Gareth and I discuss the nature of 'battlefields', why earth that has been fought over is different.

We have lunch in Albert, glad of the warmth after three hours in the January cold.

At dusk we head to Delville Wood. This place is a real inspiration for *Dusk* and is the place that Gareth and I talk most about from our first visit. More than any other it feels like a living memorial, the trees standing in for the dead. It is still and silent of human noise... we stand apart from one another, quiet, in our own thoughts as the sun slowly fades and the darkness takes over.

9/1/18

Awake at 5:30 UK time to see the dawn at
Delville Wood. No wind. Stillness. Crows waking
up and light coming up fast. Tired. Cold. Finding
it hard to concentrate, my mind wandering off
on paths of its own.

I walk up and down a trench in the dark and
think about how this brutal atmosphere must
affect the mood of a soldier. If I'd been here for
days and weeks on end, I'd have been severely
depressed. It's when the little things – hot drinks,
soft beds, decent food – are missing that life can
seem unforgiving and cruel.

We visit Lochnagar Crater. Gareth and I came
here in 2013 and there's a film of the explosion
on YouTube. I can't remember the exact figure
but thousands were killed in a single moment
and it could be heard in England. Pleased to find
memorials to peace and to women as well as
the fallen soldiers. A brief mention of 306. This
is interesting and unusual because the Somme
region is generally silent about the executions.

We visit Theipval memorial, a massive and
stunning Sir Edward Lutyens design, set on
a slight hill above miles and miles of flat
landscape. It's a memorial to the 72,000 missing

(those soldiers who do not have another grave).
Harry Farr's (executed in 1916) as well as HH
Munro (better known as the short-story writer
Saki). Matt records the sound of the flagpoles in
the wind, like chimes or very slow clocks.

29/1/18

First day on the words.

I've been thinking about starting this play for
ages. I had an idea of the first image for a while
but I've been holding back and letting other
ideas take their place. Plays are never just one
idea, they are a mess of ideas, put into the best
possible order. Starting a play is all about setting
the right tone, the right energy. If I can get the
beginning right then the rest will follow.

There's a truth too: starting a play is a lot easier
than *worrying about* starting a play.

Get some words down on the page and you can
sort them out later.

3/2/18

End of the first week of writing.

All the characters are talking and the story has
begun. I always love this bit. I love hearing the

characters speak for the first time, finding out what they care about, what makes them tick. I also love dropping clues or images that I will come back too later.

Of course it's a total mess and perhaps none of what I've written so far will end up in the final version. I don't care right now. The thing is to get words down on paper.

5/2/18

On my desk, amongst other things, I have a copy of *On Killing* and *What To Expect When You're Expecting.*

Research throws up strange juxtapositions.

27/2/18

Almost finished the first draft. I'm handing it to Gareth and Wils tomorrow. I'm excited to see what they make of it. I made quite a big change this morning but one that I think will work.

I've really enjoyed the writing of this first draft. A lot of writers I know say they hate the first draft but I think it's my favourite. Everything is new and exciting and you don't know where you're going to end up. It's not about polish and finish but about possibilities and ideas and mess.

Writing *Dusk* has been a series of surprises and I
feel like a different writer having completed it.

12/3/18

First day of music. Just concepts and dreams.

We dream of a school choir.

We dream of crows and church bells and
cannons.

We dream of lists.

2/4/18

Back to writing the text after a month off. I feel
distant from it, a stranger. Re-introducing myself
to the characters again while having to develop
and shape them is odd. I am methodical and
start the new draft with a new file, writing every
word out again. It's long and slow but, for me,
it's the only way to make the thing whole.

Reading *The Art of War* by Sun-Tzu:

'Master Sun said:

War is
A grave affair of state;
It is a place
Of life and death,

A road
To survival and extinction,
A matter
To be pondered carefully.'

It could be a mantra for the trilogy!

11/4/18

Hard week on the words, amongst a lot of other 'life' stuff. Trying to chisel out some concentrated time to focus on the words when there's so many distractions is now the job of writers (and maybe it always was).

One of the challenges of the form I've chosen (the direct address) is that each speech is like a block of wood, specifically carved to fit this part of the story. What happens when I notice it's in the wrong place is that I have to dismantle all the pieces around it and build the whole story back up again, sanding and chipping away, until everything fits.

That's the long way round to say that it is both heavy lifting and incredibly fiddly.

Wils and Cecile (designer) have an idea about a gardener which is confusing to me at this point in time but might be beautiful if I can find a way to access it.

I love all of Cecile's sketches and Wils is constantly coming up with new ideas. As challenging as I find it to remain constantly open to others while writing my own vision and within my own limits, this is the dream. Brilliant brains making beautiful things with your words.

After writing the above and obviously in a poetic mood, I found this by Kevin Powers (poet and veteran of Iraq). It's from *Death, Mother and Child*:

'The truth has no spare mercy, see. It is this chisel in the woodblock. It is this black wisp above the music of a twice-rung bell.'

I love the images here although I feel they are very personal to Powers, their music and tone speak to me too.

22/5/18

Everything except the beginning and the list is in the bin. A fresh page.

It's not quite true, there are things that I'm keeping. The essentials of the major characters are there but pretty much all the words have to be junked.

This happened with *Dawn* and it happened with *Day*. It's not what you dream of. Especially on a project with a tight time frame.

The temptation is to play it safe from this point onwards, to stick to what you know.

I feel like I can't play it safe.

I think that safe is probably what got me into this mess in the first place.

27/5/18

2 years ago we opened *Dawn* in the Pitcairn Farm outside Perth at 2:30 a.m.

It feels like yesterday and forever ago.

28/5/18

Writing a lot and cutting more.

I'm attempting to draw out as much drama in as short a space as possible.

Also building space for songs and image.

It's something I forget but our brains are hardwired for story and you often only need a suggestion to build a whole world.

I reckon that Rachel and Keith are approaching completion. Harris needs work. His story is based on fact but I need to delve into it.

There's not long to go before development but I'm trying to be playful nonetheless. Draft due at the end of the week.

7/6/18

First day of 2-day development.

All new plays are given time in development when we try out what we have with actors in a rehearsal room. This development is very close to our first week's rehearsal in July so there's slightly more pressure to make some big discoveries but everyone seems optimistic.

Joshua Miles (who played Willie in *Dawn*) is back to read Harris and it's lovely to have someone in the room who already has knowledge of the material.

We also have Cecile (designer) and Lu Kemp (dramaturg) with us.

The reading goes well and the list takes 10 minutes to read and leaves everyone exhausted. I wasn't sure whether it landed as it should but the room is enthusiastic and moved by it. One of the first times in history these names have been read out, I imagine.

Lots of notes and questions follow. Development is tough on the playwright. It's great to have the opportunity to make the play better but it can be bruising to have so many people pulling the text apart.

But I know the play intimately now so I'm able to listen and take notes and absorb.

The whole team go for dinner in the evening and we talk about *Love Island*. At the end of a hard day discussing warfare and death, it's exactly what we need.

27/6/18

Good dramaturgy session with Wils. We imagined what Shakespeare play *Dusk* would be (*Winter's Tale*) and how to describe it to a primitive warlord (the community is sick so 3 strangers are chosen to go into the woods to find answers).

I feel like we are getting closer to what this play is for each of us and what its possibilities are.

Rehearsals start on Monday.

2/7/18

First day of rehearsals.

I want to enjoy the feeling of having reached the point. Just to get here feels amazing.

In 2013, when Gareth and I first pitched this trilogy, it felt impossible. A trilogy!? You're having a laugh, pal! Trilogies were something that other people did, *proper writers.*

But here we are.

Fucking hell.

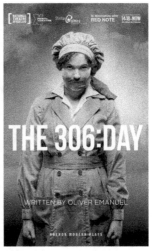

Printed in the USA
CPSIA information can be obtained
at www.ICGtesting.com
LVHW020854171024
794056LV00002B/525

9 781786 826282